C000291963

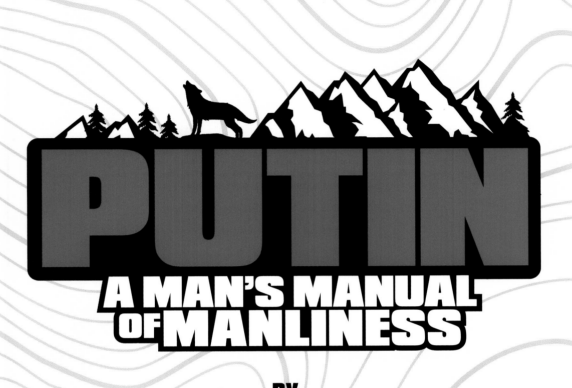

# PUTIN
## A MAN'S MANUAL OF MANLINESS

BY
EDWARD RAINSHED

PORTICO

This is an independent publication. It is completely unofficial
and unauthorised and, as such, has no connection with the people
or persons featured, or with any organisation or individual connected
in any way whatsoever with the people or persons featured.

First published in the United Kingdom in 2019 by
Portico
43 Great Ormond Street
London
WC1N 3HZ

An imprint of Pavilion Books Company Ltd

Copyright © Pavilion Books Company Ltd 2019
Text copyright © Yes/No Publishing Services 2019

All rights reserved. No part of this publication may be copied,
displayed, extracted, reproduced, utilised, stored in a retrieval system
or transmitted in any form or by any means, electronic, mechanical or
otherwise including but not limited to photocopying, recording,
or scanning without the prior written permission of the publishers.

ISBN 978-1-91162-233-8

A CIP catalogue record for this book
is available from the British Library.

10 9 8 7 6 5 4 3 2 1

Reproduction by Rival Colour Ltd, UK
Printed and bound by 1010 Printing International Ltd, China

This book can be ordered direct from the publisher at
www.pavilionbooks.com

MIX
Paper from
responsible sources
FSC® C016973

# AN INTRODUCTION

Sept 10th, 2019

Dear Reader,

For more than a decade now, there have been rumours surrounding the existence of a secret study into the nature of masculinity – a series of handwritten notes, typed documents and various artifacts and ephemera – purportedly written and curated by the Russian President, Vladimir Putin.

I have spent many years searching for this fabled dossier of work. But at every turn, the scent has gone cold.

And then, in the fall of 2018, I received a mysterious notification to follow a link to the 'dark web', where I discovered a folder of anonymous notes written by a mystery Russian action man. Could this be the legendary manual of manliness from the mind of Vladimir Vladimirovich Putin himself?

After months of in-depth research, adamant denials from my sources in the Kremlin, and a need to pay my mortgage, I have decided to release my findings, despite being unable to ascertain the writer's true identity. And thus, I present to you these fascinating and often poignant documents, alongside hand-picked, authenticated quotes from arguably the most powerful man in the world. Fake news or Putin's own *A Man's Manual of Manliness*? Judge for yourselves…

Yours truly

Edward Rainshed
(in hiding)

"I think happiness is love."

VLADIMIR VLADIMIROVICH PUTIN

## MASTERING PAIN

Pain can be your enemy but there are times when pain can also be your bedfellow. If you allow pain to take control of you, it will infect you like a cankerous sore. Pain can undermine you both physically and mentally. But when conquered, pain can inspire and motivate you to achieve great things.

To become immune to pain, you must first keep it as a constant companion. Hide gravel in your shoe or bathe yourself in scalding water. Conceal a peach stone between your buttocks and continue your day – do these things and you will swiftly discover how relentless discomfort and abrasion of your soft tissue can focus you like nothing else. Refuse anaesthetics during dental procedures.

Soon you will learn to become one with pain. If you treat pain like a beautiful bird — love it and nurture it – then, one day, pain will fly within you and you will become pain's master.

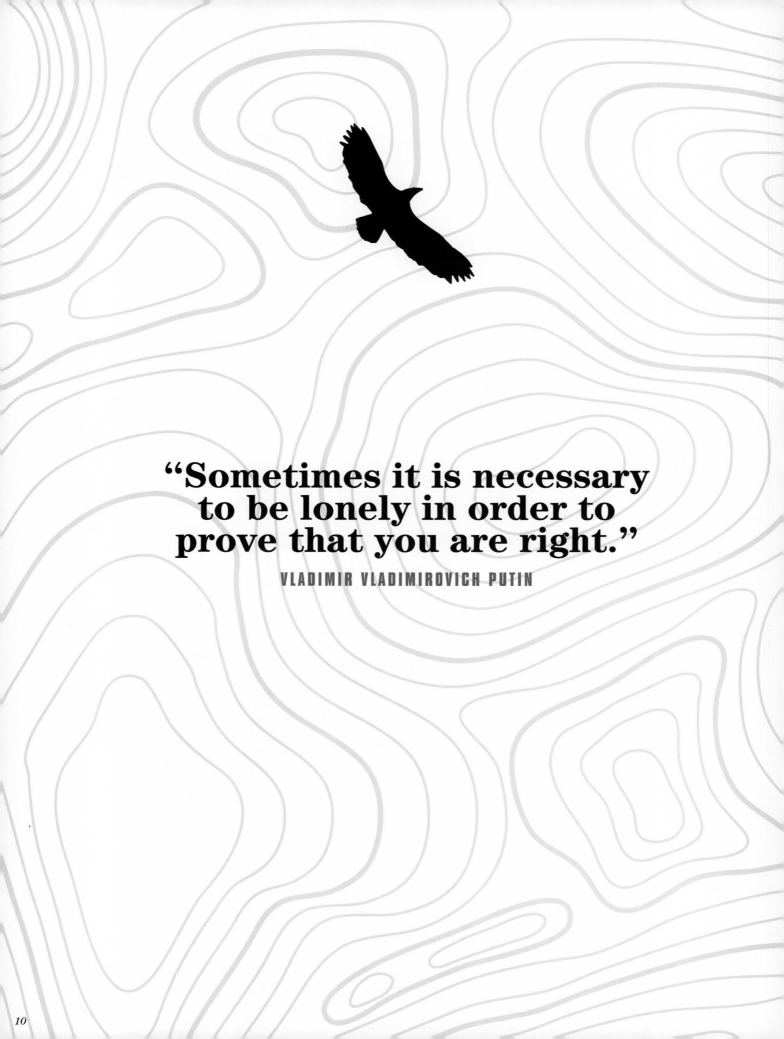

> **"Sometimes it is necessary to be lonely in order to prove that you are right."**
>
> VLADIMIR VLADIMIROVICH PUTIN

## HORSEMANSHIP

I continue my studies into the nature of horses. It is my belief that, by better understanding horses, I will better understand myself.

Consider the beauty of a horse in motion. Notice the light ripple across the glossy rump, the delicate fetlocks arched and poised, like a prima ballerina. The equine musculature is graceful, powerful, hypnotic, sensual.

Like great men, horses are strong, yet sensitive. The harsh leather of a saddle, for example, can chafe delicate ribs. This can be soothed by gently rubbing oils into the hide or prevented altogether by riding bareback, naked as nature intended.

It is important to understand that your relationship with a horse is not one of master and beast, but of two equals working in partnership, one atop the other.

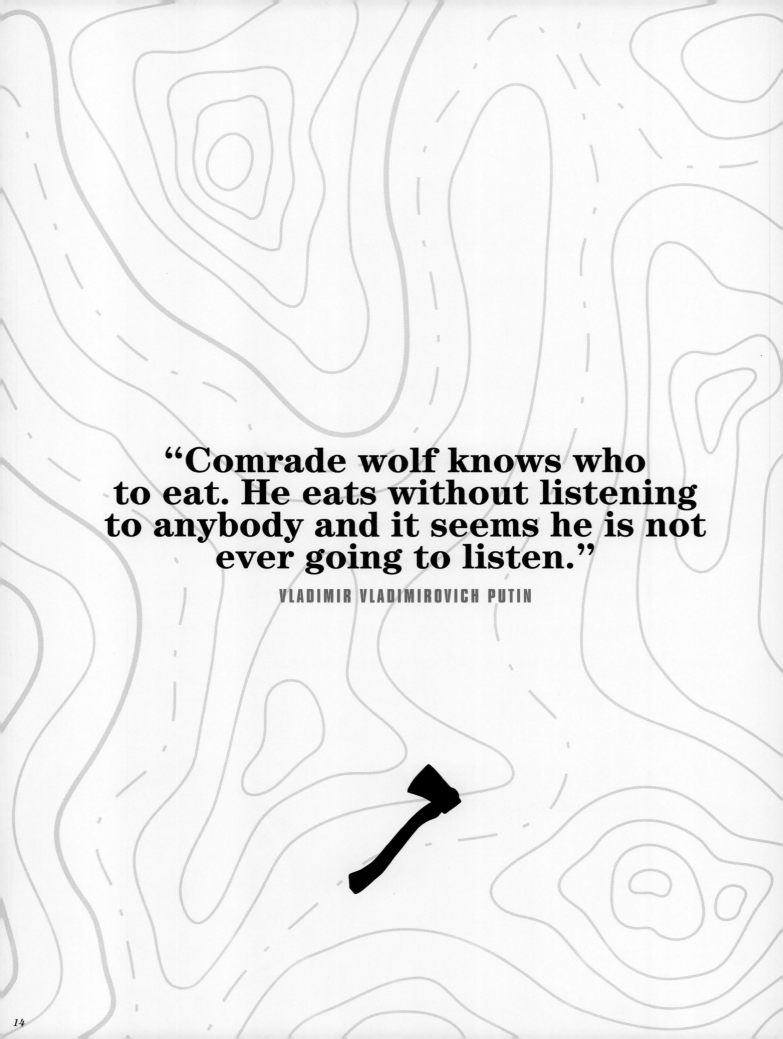

"Comrade wolf knows who to eat. He eats without listening to anybody and it seems he is not ever going to listen."

VLADIMIR VLADIMIROVICH PUTIN

HOW TO TACKLE A BEAR

Like people, bears will submit to an aggressive show of bravado designed to demonstrate who is boss. Many times I have encountered mighty beasts and stood them down with my domineering body stance and ten million yard stare.

Here is my checklist of tips to take down an angry bear.

REMAIN CALM AND COMPOSED - make measured movements, like those of a black belt judo master

ANNOUNCE YOURSELF - exclaim confidently, "I AM MAN AND I WILL OVERCOME"

SET YOUR STARE - channel the ice dams and glacial lakes of Siberia

In one seamless motion rip off your shirt to reveal your impressive toned chest and bulging biceps.

The bear should now have backed off.

If that is not the case command one of your bodyguards to shoot the bear between the eyes.

# "It is extremely dangerous to encourage people to see themselves as exceptional, whatever the motivation."

VLADIMIR VLADIMIROVICH PUTIN

## MASCULINE SMELLS

A man's scent defines his masculinity, but the modern trend is to disguise one's natural scent with artificial perfumes. A floral-scented man may have the heart of an aesthete, while a citrus-scented man may have a sharp wit, but a bitter demeanour.

However, a man who smells of sweat, leather and smoke is truly male. It is possible to enhance the masculinity of your odour with external scents. If you do not smoke yourself, you can adopt a smoky scent by spending many hours in the smoking areas of a vodka room, or by sleeping overnight in a herring smokery. Dress yourself entirely in leather and the oils from the leather will be absorbed into your own skin, augmenting your own bodily fragrance.

Do not wash. Your perspiration is a key element of your natural musk, which is essential for telegraphing masculinity to other males or to a potential mate. If you are not a naturally sweaty person, you may also amplify your virility by harvesting musk from the musk pods of the Siberian musk deer.

"There is no such thing as a former KGB man."

VLADIMIR VLADIMIROVICH PUTIN

(fig. 1)

(fig. 2)

(fig. 3)

(fig. 4)

(fig. 5)

ROUGH-HOUSING

Camaraderie with colleagues and friends can be hard to achieve.
I find that friendly wrestling can often break the ice. But
friendliness must not be confused with weakness.

I have developed rough-housing techniques that can be utilised
around the workplace. They are particularly effective when used in
conjunction with the element of surprise. Much fun for all!

At a summit of world leaders, disguise your intentions with a firm
handshake, then wrap your body around your opponent's upper torso
and engage the foreign dignitary in THE HUMILIATION OF THE
COSSACK (fig. 1). You will have the room laughing instantly.

A subordinate has failed in their duty. Lighten the mood by
grabbing one arm, then one leg. Now spin them around and release
them so they skid across the floor. I have named this manoeuvre THE
REVERSE FLYING TSAR (fig. 2). Laughter whilst performing this move
adds an extra layer of good humour.

Sneak up behind your friend/victim and wrap your arms around their
stomach, interlocking your fingers so they cannot break free. Now
perform THE KIEV CHICKEN (fig. 3) by squeezing their soft innards
until they release bile.

Tensions are high around the negotiating table. Unannounced, leap
from your chair and engage your colleague in THE HUMAN KNOT (fig.
4) and hold until submission. All frictions will be dissipated.

The diplomatic process has reached a stalemate. Neither side is
budging. In one smooth motion, lift your foot and give your opponent
A FIRM KICK IN THE BALTICS (fig. 5).

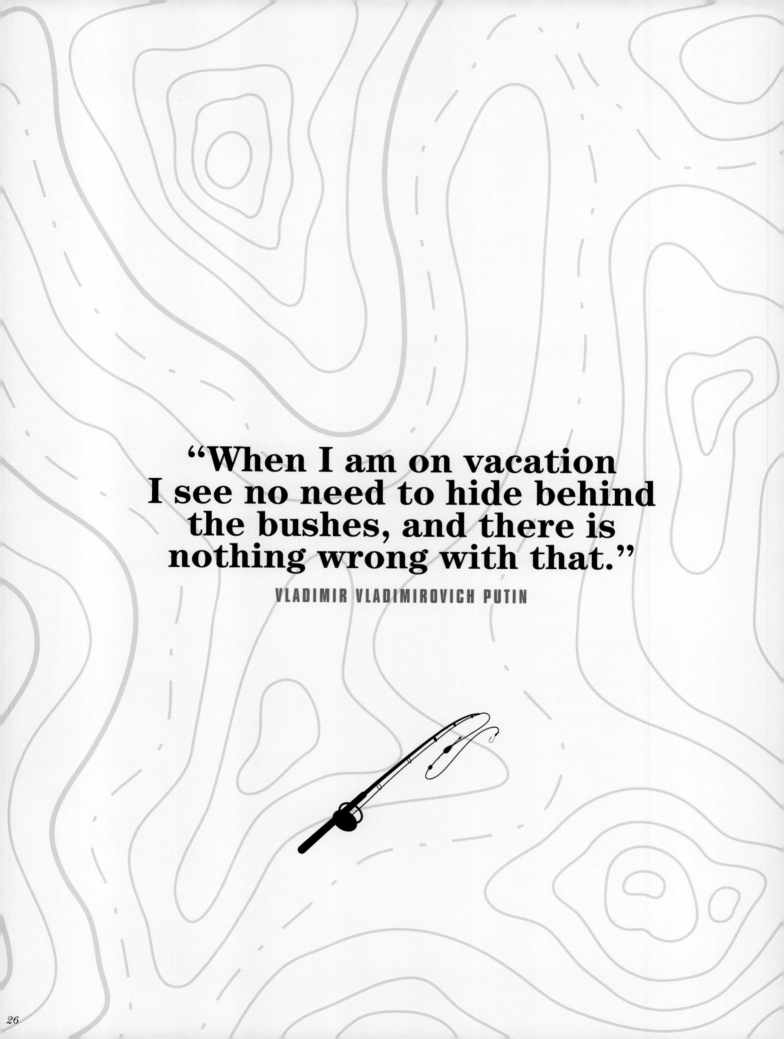

"When I am on vacation
I see no need to hide behind
the bushes, and there is
nothing wrong with that."

VLADIMIR VLADIMIROVICH PUTIN

## FORAGING TO STAY ALIVE

Being able to find the nourishment to maintain life is an essential skill. A man should be able sustain himself by harvesting from the natural world around him: berries, nettles, fungi, spiky thorns and nuts. Essential fluids can be gathered from the waterfalls, natural springs, the morning dew and, in extreme situations, from one's own urine, filtered through moss.

## FORAGING FOR FUN

You can forage anywhere – even at work. For example, at a diplomatic soiree, you may wish to reject the food provided by the official caterers for fear of poisoning, and instead forage for mints, gum or boiled sweets about your person. Failing that, pocket lint and paper receipts contain basic nutrients that can support life and quell hunger pangs.

**"I do not think I am ready to wear the laurel of ‹the coolest man in politics›, and actually I do not find anything out of the ordinary in my work in conservation or my active lifestyle. In my opinion, both things are normal for anyone."**

VLADIMIR VLADIMIROVICH PUTIN

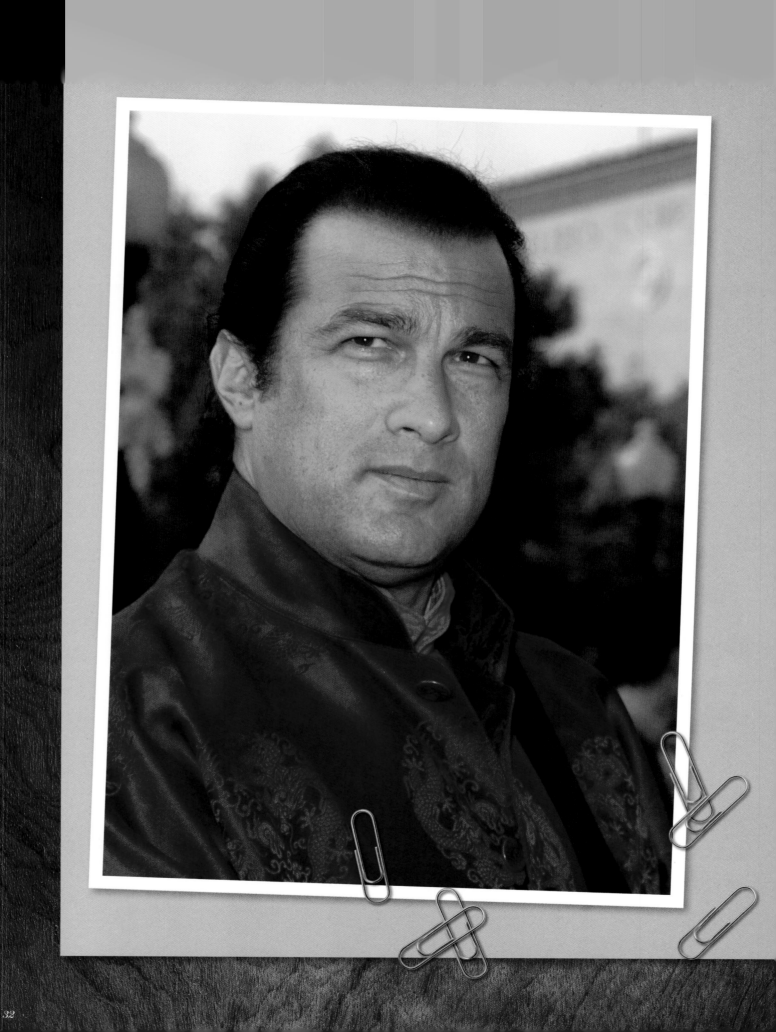

STEVEN

Bathing in a lake and wrestling in a forest
Steven
A friend to a man and a man who is a friend
Steven
Soaring through the sky or in my mind's eye
Steven
Speaking without words for words are not enough
Steven
A companion in my heart and beside my hearth
Steven
With the will of a stallion and the roar of a jaguar
Steven
Stubborn as a mountain but crazy like a catfish
Steven
A raven-haired judo angel come to save my soul
Steven
Hard to Kill and never Under Siege
Steven
Steven
Steve

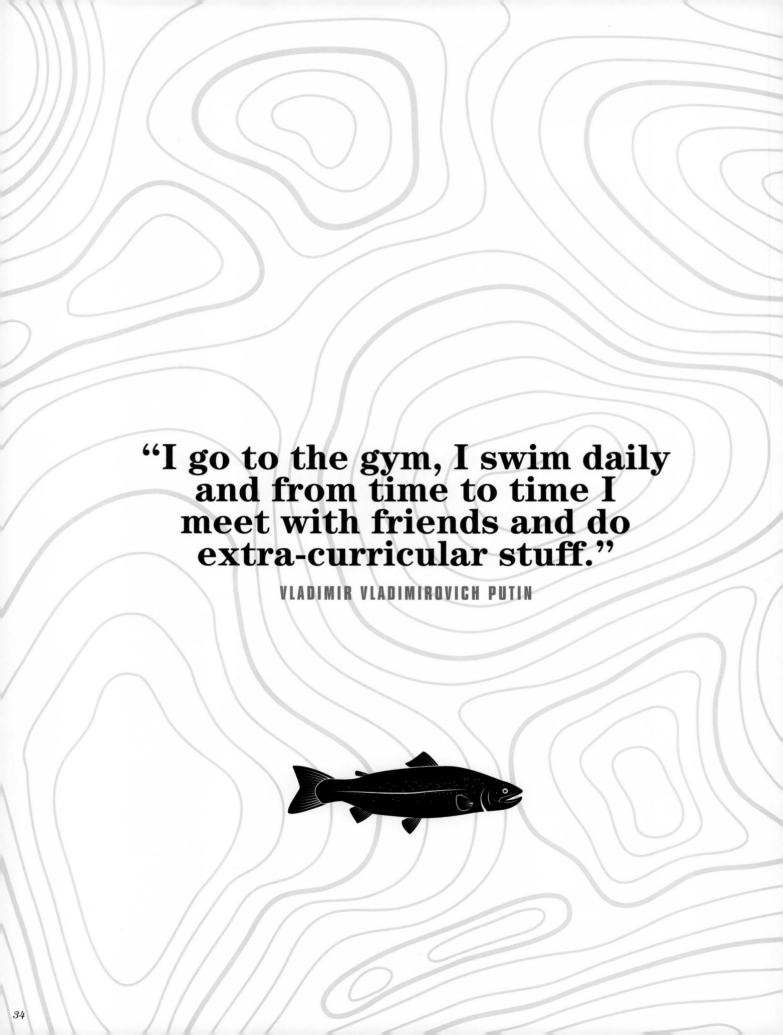

"I go to the gym, I swim daily and from time to time I meet with friends and do extra-curricular stuff."

# ICE BATHS

Bathing in ice stimulates the skin and speeds up recovery after exercise. There are a variety of places to take ice baths, both in the city and in the wild. Submerge your body fully under the water and see how long you can remain there for. A hyper-fit sixty-six-year-old man should be able to withstand up to ten minutes submerged in water 32.5°F (0.3°C) before losing consciousness. Anything less is weakness.

After an ice bath, it can be beneficial to gargle 'tree water', the naturally cleansing sap of the birch tree.

In Oymyakon, some say the coldest place in Russia, the ice bath has been known to stimulate hair growth in bald men.

Strong men can make lasting bonds of friendship in an ice bath – unwavering fronds of loyalty.

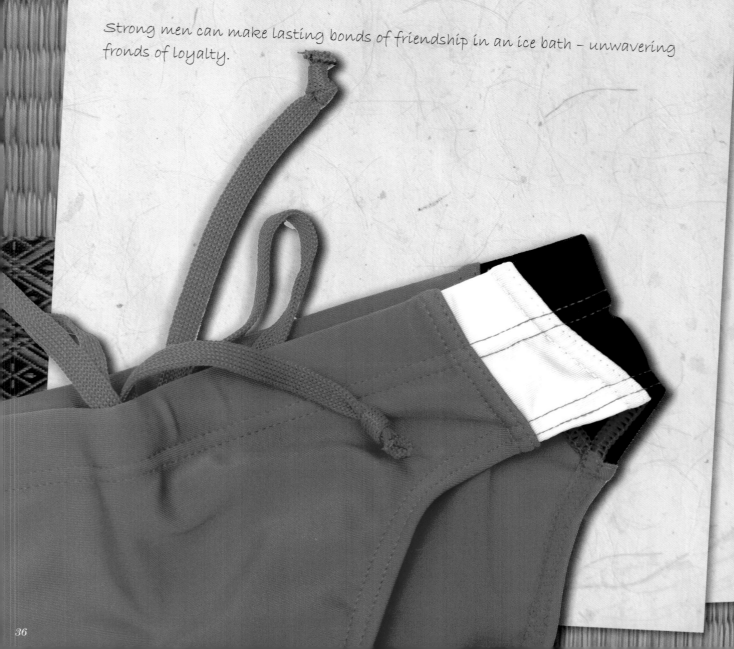

"Let me tell you something – there is no need to fear Russia."

VLADIMIR VLADIMIROVICH PUTIN

## HIDING IN PLAIN SIGHT

I am able to make myself entirely undetectable to the human eye. I have become a master of blending into my surroundings like a wild cheetah stalking its prey.

The most effective way to do this is to make yourself so irrefutably visible that you become completely invisible. The key is to cleverly deflect the perception filters of the weak-minded so that they believe you are not, in fact, there.

To become invisible, cunningly redirect people's attentions by casually pointing out something that will distract them – a nearby pigeon, for example, or badger.

With attention successfully diverted, take the opportunity to become your surroundings. Concentrate hard. If, in your very core, you believe that you are a fridge, you will be that fridge.

These techniques can be employed in any situation: whilst hunting game, for example, or during a diplomatic dinner, or at a discotheque.

"I have worked like a galley slave throughout these eight years, morning till night, and I have given all I could to this work. I am happy with the results."

VLADIMIR VLADIMIROVICH PUTIN

## MUSIC

Music is a muse, it can sedate and excite. But music isn't just Bruce Hornsby and the Range or Chris de Burgh or Marillion. Music can be made at any time and in any situation.

With the right tools you can make a musical instrument from your surroundings – even a flute from a branch!

First it is important to learn to know branches. This can take many, many years but once mastered you'll choose correctly every time. Dry, straight branches with few knots are best. Imagining you are the branch will help when understanding the best way to carve it. With your hunting knife or sabre cut the branch to no shorter than 15cm in length. Now drill a hole lengthways through the branch using a tiger tooth. Using a sharpened fish spine drill 5 holes into the branch, approximately 2cm apart. Now you have a flute.

Other instruments you can fashion from nature include a wild-boar-bladder bagpipe, a badger-ribcage xylophone and mushroom bongos.

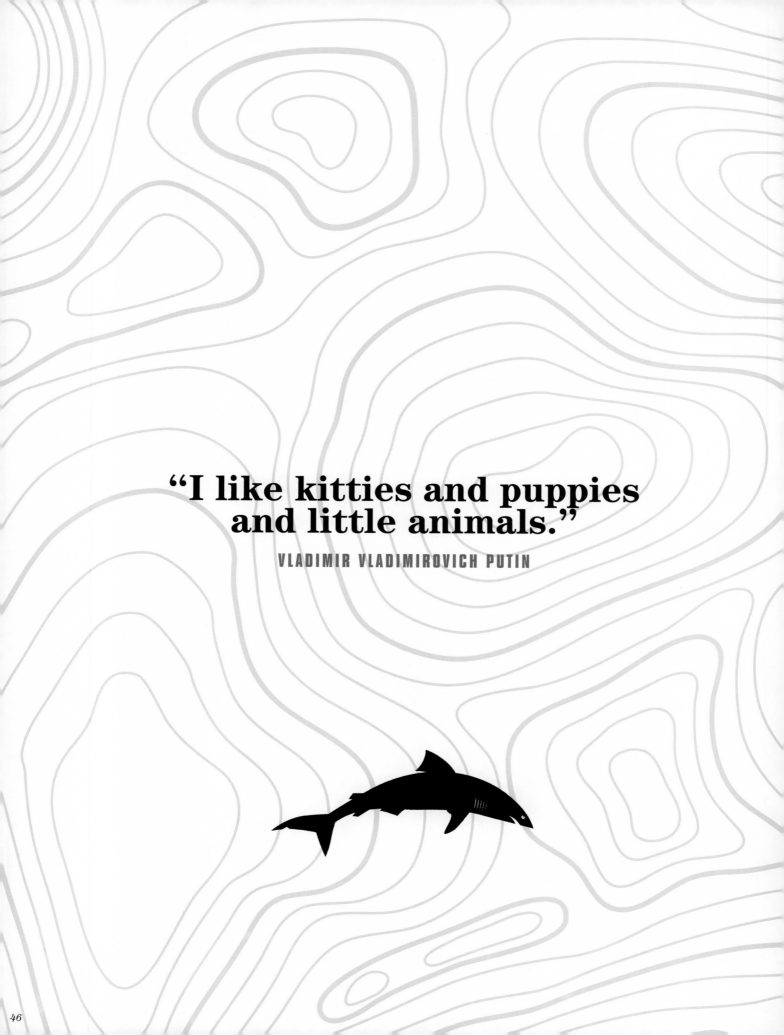

"I like kitties and puppies and little animals."

VLADIMIR VLADIMIROVICH PUTIN

## CRYING

It is a mistake to assume that weeping is a weakness. Sadness and grief are powerful natural emotions and it is possible for a man to draw immense strength from his own tears.

However, the most potent tears of all are the ones that fall inside your body, not the ones that run down your cheeks. Thus, I have devised methods of crying within.

At the funeral of a close friend or colleague, for instance, it is possible to keep your tears in by imagining that the deceased ally was actually an enemy, who was planning to betray you all along.

Retain your dignity during moments of great tragedy by staring ahead and silently humming a cheerful tune – 'Walking on Sunshine' by Katrina and the Waves, perhaps, or 'Girls Just Want to Have Fun' by Cyndi Lauper.

<u>Remember – emotions will never undermine your masculinity as long as you do not display them to others.</u>

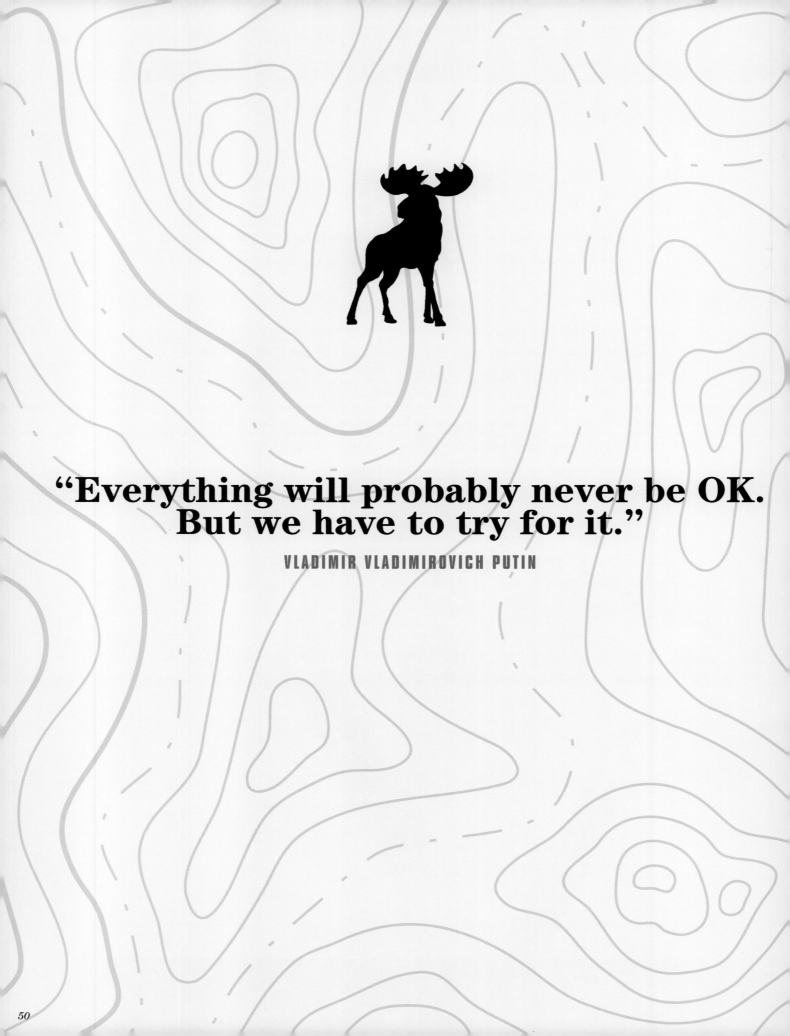

"Everything will probably never be OK.
But we have to try for it."

VLADIMIR VLADIMIROVICH PUTIN

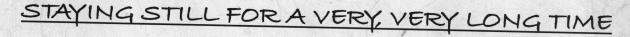

# STAYING STILL FOR A VERY, VERY LONG TIME

Sometimes it is necessary to remain totally still. I consider it to be an essential skill that can soothe a reticent orphan child, impress a visiting dignitary or maybe even save your life.

## SITUATIONS WHERE IT MAY BE RELEVANT TO STAY STILL FOR A VERY, VERY LONG TIME:

- When hunting
- When negotiating at a political summit
- When considering prose
- When pretending to be a statue
- When hiding in a trunk for many hours while your enemy surrounds you
- When facing the world's press
- When pretending to be dead
- When hiding from a stag
- When surveying your kingdom from atop a mountain

## IT TAKES MANY YEARS TRAINING TO BE ABLE TO STAY STILL FOR A VERY, VERY LONG TIME. SOME PEOPLE ARE NEVER ABLE TO ATTAIN TRUE STILLNESS.
## TO ACHIEVE A STILL STATE YOU MUST:

1. Empty your mind of all matters however imperative
2. Slow down your heart to less than 10 beats per minute
3. Stare a thousand years into the future
4. Imagine your body to have been carved from the Ural Mountains
5. Lower your body temperature to -25 degrees centigrade
6. Mentally regress to the womb
7. Plant your feet on the ground as if you were hewn of Siberian Fir
8. Make all movements internally, live inside yourself
9. Stay very, very, very, very still

# "The more I know about people, the more I like dogs. I simply like animals."

VLADIMIR VLADIMIROVICH PUTIN

PUPPIES

Man and dog have lived in close union for many centuries. The bond
between a man and his dog is a primal connection. In many ways, dogs
are more reliable and better companions than humans. They offer
unwavering loyalty, unconditional love and warmth in cold climates.

Train a dog when he is young and malleable, and you will be able to
manipulate his nature and force him to do your bidding - attack
an angry mob of protesters, sniff out traitors, or carry official
documentation across hundreds of miles of icy tundra.

# Cute Puppies

🔍

All · Images · Videos · Shopping · News · More · Settings · Tools · 📑 Collections · SafeSearch

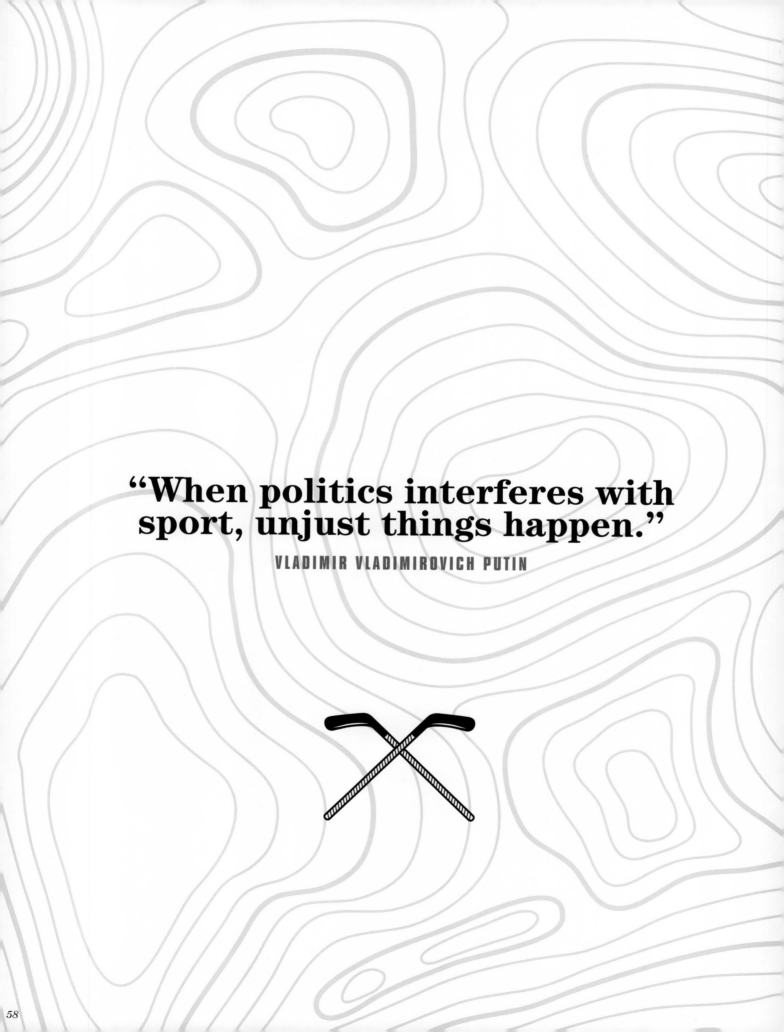

# "When politics interferes with sport, unjust things happen."

VLADIMIR VLADIMIROVICH PUTIN

HEMP

JUTE

WOOL

SISAL

NYLON

# FAVOURITE TWINES

## HEMP

Versatile and attractive, hemp twine can be delicate enough to weave the finest macramé adornments, yet strong enough to bind the wrists of your worst enemies.

## JUTE

A tough natural fibre, jute twine can be used for tying dried boar meat together, or for crafting hessian garments when you need to disguise yourself (e.g., as a peasant, or monk).

## WOOL

A soft, warm, flaxen yarn. Always keep a shearing knife upon your person – you never know when you may need to relieve a sheep, bison or alpaca of its fleece.

## SISAL

Produces a stiff, unyielding twine that does not attract dust, and is thus ideal for hunters, trappers, action film stars and other tough, outdoor types who suffer from allergies.

## NYLON

A light, man-made twine composed of fine, synthetic fibres, nylon's superior strength makes it perfect for everything from reeling in an obstinate sturgeon to garrotting a flailing mink.

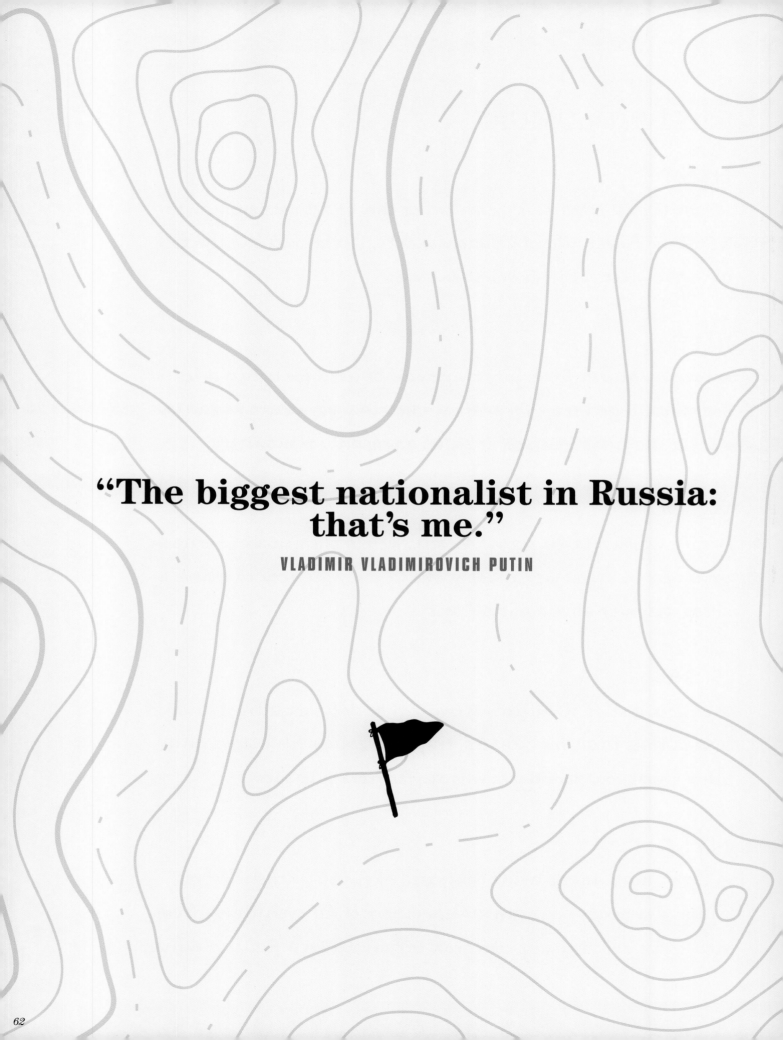

# "The biggest nationalist in Russia: that's me."

VLADIMIR VLADIMIROVICH PUTIN

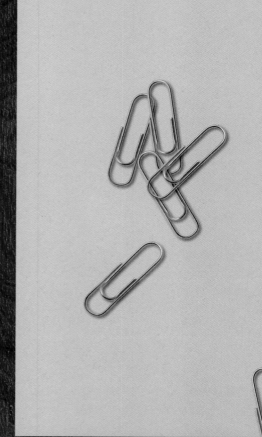

VODKA

Vodka is an integral part of Russian culture. It warms your body and warms your soul. But vodka isn't just for drinking. Few people realise the full potential of this miracle liquid.

Vodka has restorative properties. You may, for instance, revive a stunned salmon by dabbing a small drop of vodka on its lips. Vodka is also highly flammable and can be used to cook the salmon (if you were unable to revive it).

Vodka is one of the few fluids that can act as both an anaesthetic and a disinfectant. Applied to a wound it can prevent infection. And, when consumed orally in sufficient quantities, it can deaden pain, allowing you to sew your own wound up, like John Rambo in the film First Blood.

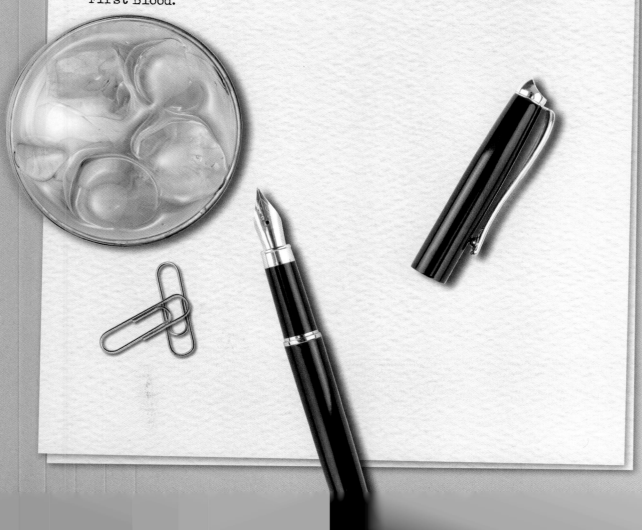

# "Berlusconi is being tried because he lives with women. If he were homosexual, no one would lift a finger against him."

VLADIMIR VLADIMIROVICH PUTIN

## SOLITUDE

A man can never truly understand himself until he is completely alone. Prolonged periods of solitude can strengthen your character and sharpen your instincts.

Climb the snowy peak of a high mountain and remain there for seven days, taking only water and modest provisions.

Retreat to a deserted monastery and live among the ruins in silence for up to a month.

Float alone in the Baltic Sea on a handmade raft until you push yourself to the boundaries of human sanity. When you begin to hallucinate, it is time to return to shore.

However, in our busy times, it is not always possible to escape the modern world. Instead, you can find mental isolation in any circumstance by simply retreating to your inner fortress of solitude. To others you will appear present and attentive. But in your mind you will be at peace, like a lone eagle on the wind.

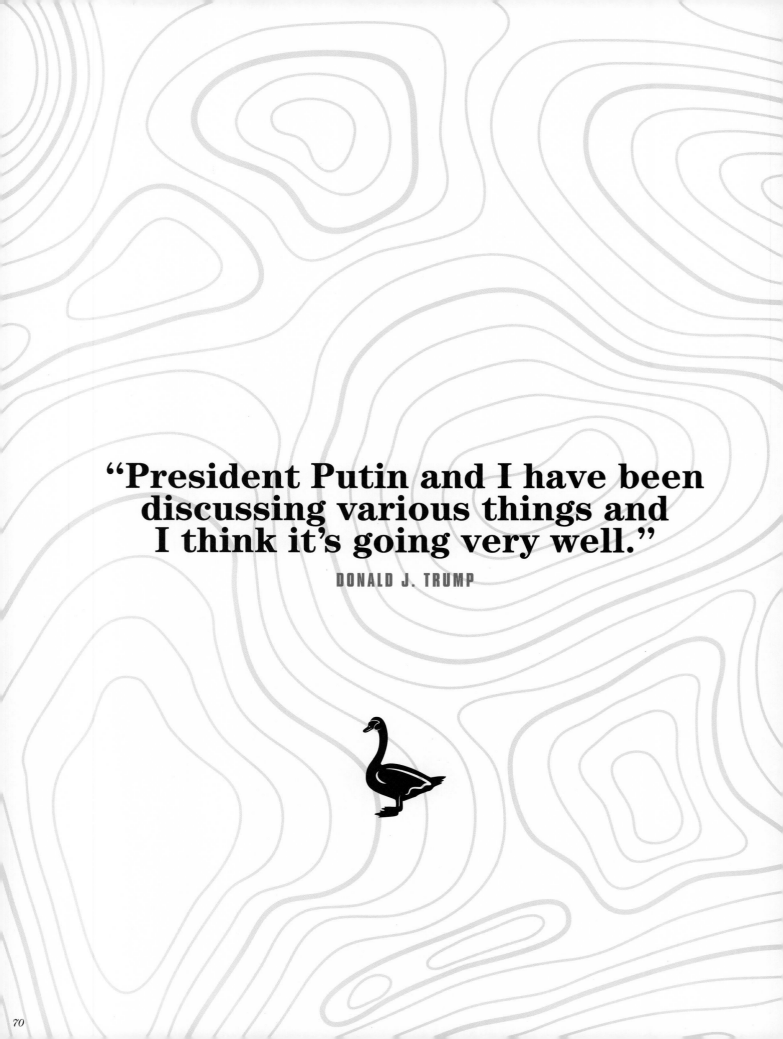

"**President Putin and I have been discussing various things and I think it's going very well.**"

DONALD J. TRUMP

## MIND CONTROL

Some say that mind control is impossible, but I know you will believe me when I say that it is possible. I know this. Soon you will know this too.

On many occasions I have used the techniques below to bend the opinions of those that wish to do me harm - be they friend or foe, human or beast.

- Imagine you are a wild Siberian tiger

- Hold your adversary's stare at all times and penetrate their eyes with unflinching steel

- Stealthily reduce the distance between yourself and your adversary whilst cooing gently to soothe any fear away

- With calmness and precision clasp your adversary's head between your hands (claws)

- Exert mild pressure on their ears whilst maintaining eye contact

- Gently blow up your adversary's nostrils until their eyes widen

- Your adversary is now under your control

Whisper your command into your adversary's ear and have them do as you wish, but be gentle; mind control is fickle like a feisty young lover or a feather on a branch - it can be untethered by a breeze and lost forever if concentration wavers even a little.

"If a fight is inevitable,
go and fight first."

VLADIMIR VLADIMIROVICH PUTIN

## BREAKING IN A WILD MARE

First approach her in a crouching position to show your respect and deference. In low, hushed tones repeat this soothing phrase:

"Hushaling-a, hushaling-a, hushaling-a-hoe-hoe"

As you draw closer, rise up to assert your dominance and fix her with a stare. As you circle her, lift your knees as you walk, like a proud, prancing stallion.

As quick as a mongoose, leap on the horse's bare back and hold on tightly to her flowing mane. Prepare yourself for a struggle, as she bucks and writhes beneath you. Remain in situ no matter what, despite percussive trauma you may sustain to the groin and buttock area. The pain will remind you of the delicate balance between man and nature.

She is an angry mare and needs to feel your supremacy. But, once submitted, she will become docile and compliant. Now, gently stroke her flanks and sing her this calming refrain:

"Shalla-lalla-lalla-la-la-lows. Shalla-lalla-lalla-la-la-lows."

The same techniques can be employed with other animals, including elephants, camels and very large dogs.

"I think people like Mr Blatter
or the heads of big international
sporting federations, or the Olympic
Games, deserve special recognition.
If there is anyone who deserves the
Nobel Prize, it's those people."

VLADIMIR VLADIMIROVICH PUTIN

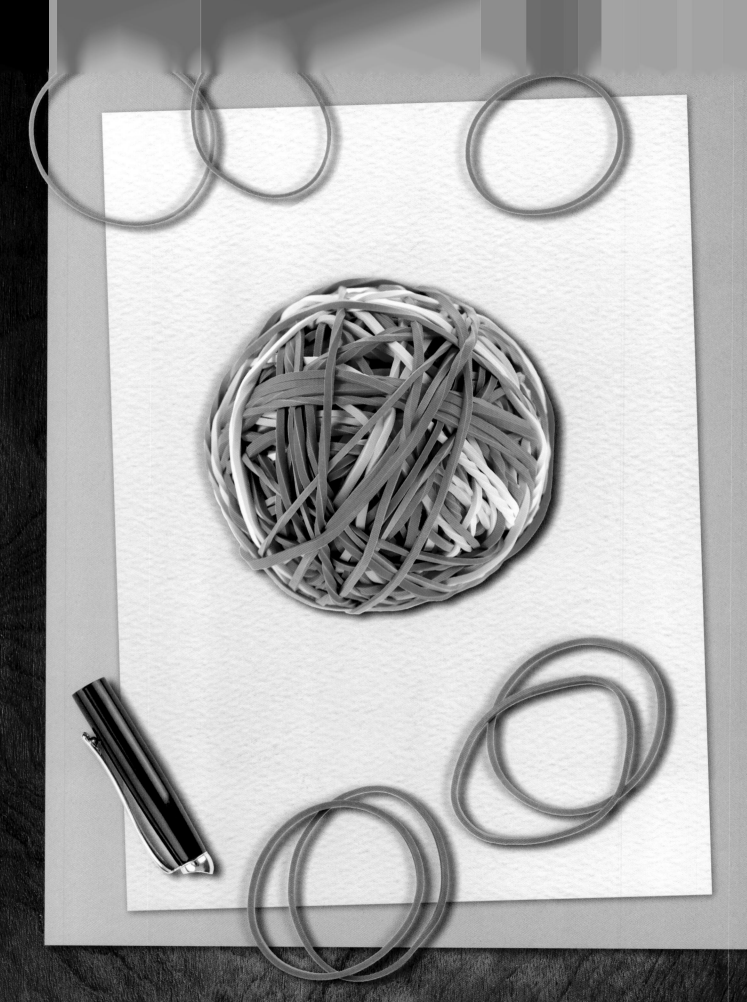

## BODY LANGUAGE

Humans communicate in many ways. It is easy to recognise verbal communication, but it is also possible to recognise the language of the body.

If someone is rubbing their neck or shoulders, then they are just anxious. You are in no danger. If, however, someone is leaning towards you with a fist raised and an angry expression, then they are a threat, especially if they are holding a knife or gun. Disarm them immediately using your judo training, or retreat.

A person who is perspiring heavily, avoiding eye contact, rubbing their nose and covering their mouth as they address you is a liar. Do not trust their words. They are probably plotting your downfall.

If another man offers his hand, it may seem like a friendly greeting. But if, during your handshake, he attempts to force your hand down so that his is on top, and he places his other hand under your elbow, then he is looking to dominate you. Reverse this, by twisting his hand sharply and pressing your thumb into the soft tissue between his thumb and forefinger, reasserting your dominance.

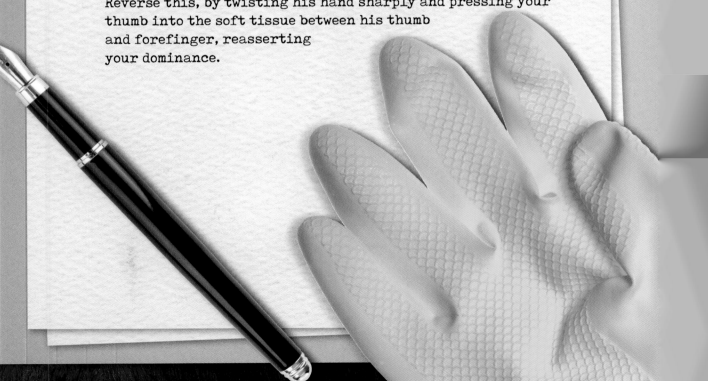

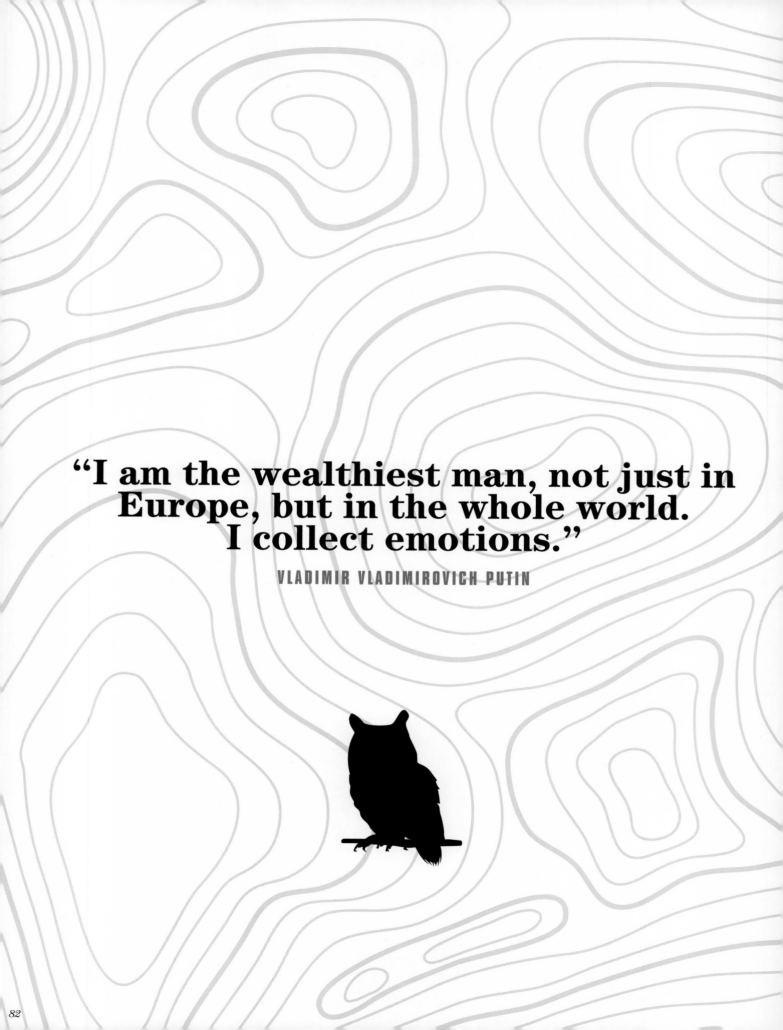

"I am the wealthiest man, not just in Europe, but in the whole world. I collect emotions."

VLADIMIR VLADIMIROVICH PUTIN

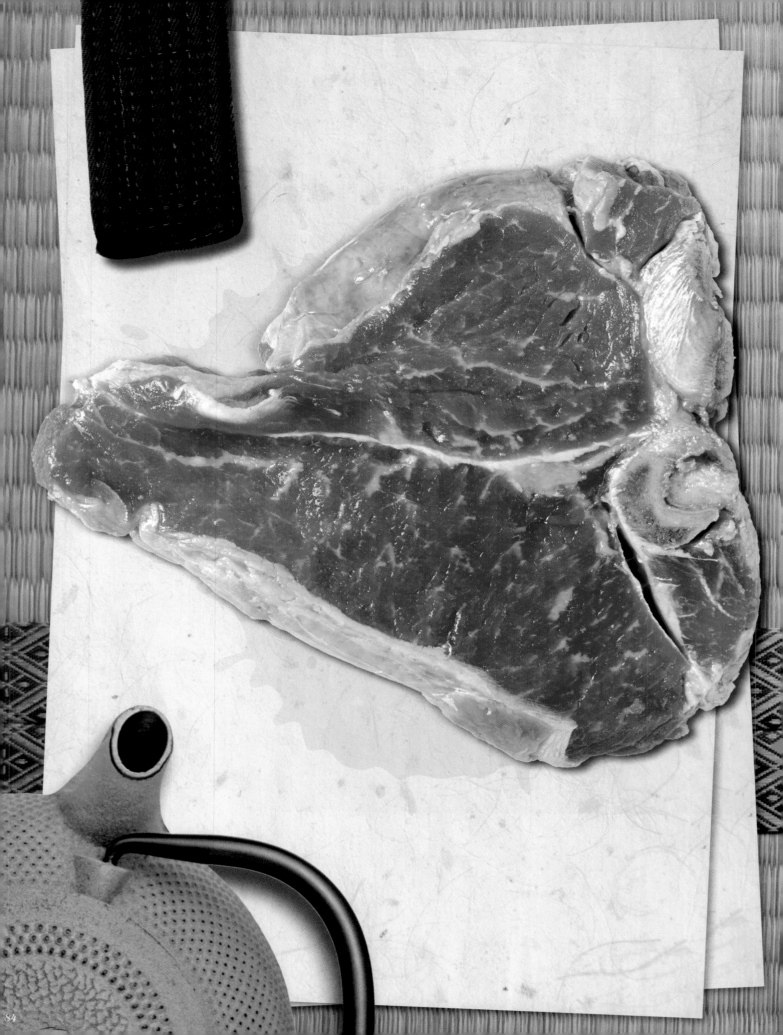

## HEALTH

An unhealthy man will never achieve greatness.

Exercise constantly. Remain physically active at all times. Even if your circumstances don't allow you to perform outward exercise, it is possible to exercise inwardly. At a press conference, for example, you could flex the muscles in your legs, arms, abdomen. Or during a colleague's funeral, you could silently clench and unclench your buttocks.

Eat healthily. A balanced diet is important. Plenty of vegetables and lots of raw meat. Avoid sugar during the week, then after church on Sunday, allow yourself to eat a raw sugar beet as a reward.

Infect yourself with many diseases and expose yourself to poisons, to raise the effectiveness of your natural antitoxins. You can become immune to anything, except your emotions.

Enhancing your mental health will keep your mind razor sharp. Whilst sleeping, keep one half of your brain active with puzzles and riddles. A lazy brain is a wasted organ.

"I looked the man in the eye. I found him to be very straightforward and trustworthy. We had a very good dialogue. I was able to get a sense of his soul; a man deeply committed to his country and the best interests of his country."

GEORGE W. BUSH

## NATURAL POISONS

Recognising natural poisons around us is as essential a skill as reading or swordplay. Eating a deadly fungus or toxic frog is highly possible when deserted on an island or stranded at the bottom of a deep quarry. But there are poisonous dangers everywhere.

Plastics are toxic to wildlife and humans. Do not consume large amounts of plastic.

Strychnine has a bitter taste so is virtually undetectable on grapefruit. Avoid grapefruit.

Apple seeds, for example, contain cyanide in very small doses. So, if you accidentally collected 10,000 apple pips, crushed them into a paste, then ingested the paste, you could easily die. Or suffer a tummy ache at the very least. Avoid apples.

In fact, everything is poisonous in large doses - even water or air. Your best option is to have your food taster to sample everything before you do. If he dies, the likelihood is that you too will die.

# "Despite all the achievements of civilisation, the human being is still one of the most vulnerable creatures on earth."

VLADIMIR VLADIMIROVICH PUTIN

## IMPROVING TOOLS

When a man has chosen solitude in the wilderness, he does not always have access to the tools he needs. That is why it is imperative to learn how to craft essential utensils and weaponry from items around you.

A heavy stone bound to a strong stick with twine can be used as a makeshift mallet. For nails, use the teeth of a wildcat. Rodents' teeth are good pins. Now you have the instruments to provide yourself with shelter, and the means to construct other tools.

If you have lost your hunting knife whilst wading through a fast-running river, climbing a ravine or gutting some carrion, fashion a replacement from a dried herring that has been sharpened along one edge.

Never forget that your most important tools are your hands. With your hands you can rip things apart, punch holes in things and caress yourself for comfort. Protect your hands with your life.

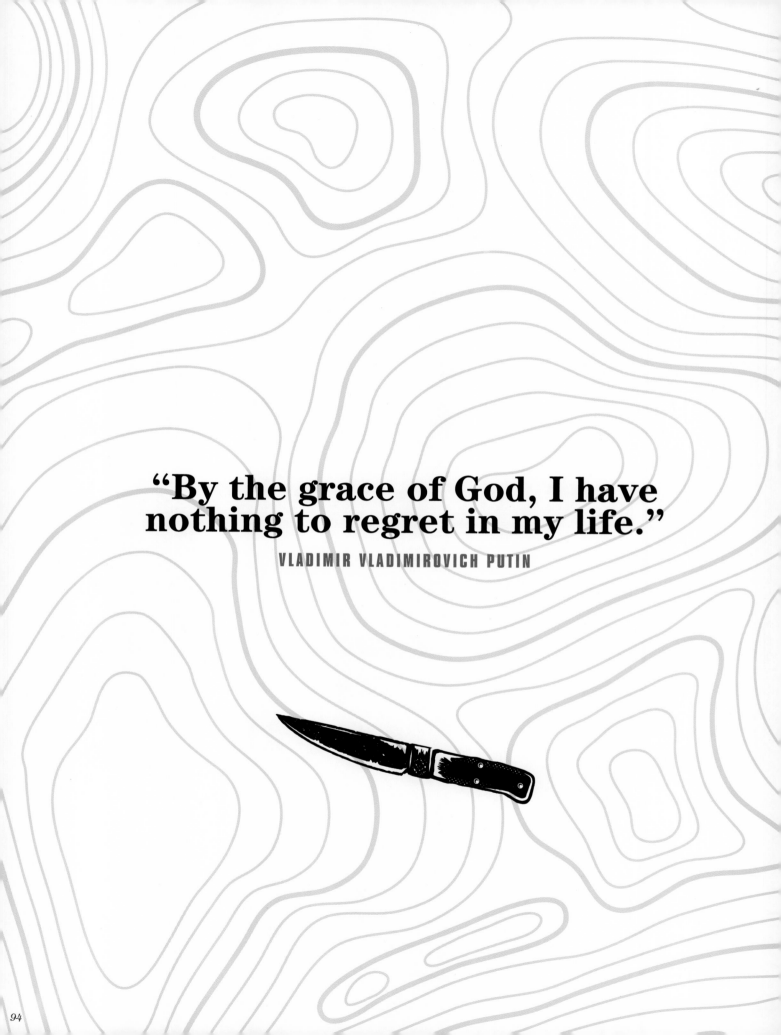

"By the grace of God, I have nothing to regret in my life."

VLADIMIR VLADIMIROVICH PUTIN

# PICTURE CREDITS

**Alamy Stock Photo:** page 7, Russian Government / Alamy Stock Photo; page 11, ITAR-TASS News Agency; page 35, Kremlin Pool / Alamy Stock Photo; page 43, Kremlin Pool / Alamy Stock Photo; page 51, Russian Government / Alamy Stock Photo; page 63, SPUTNIK / Alamy Stock Photo; page 75, ITAR-TASS News Agency / Alamy Stock Photo; page 79, ITAR-TASS News Agency / Alamy Stock Photo; page 83, SPUTNIK / Alamy Stock Photo; page 91, SPUTNIK / Alamy Stock Photo.

**Shutterstock.com:** page 32, Featureflash Photo Agency; page 37, photowind; page 41, COULANGES; page 64 (top), Willem Tims; page 64 (bottom), rnkadsgn; page 68, SimpleB; page 72, Paul Fleet; page 77, Atelier Sommerland.

**Getty Images:** page 15, Andreas Rentz/Getty Images; page 19, MIKHAIL KLIMENTYEV/AFP/Getty Images; page 23, NATALIA KOLESNIKOVA/AFP/Getty Images; page 27, Sovfoto/UIG via Getty Images; page 31, ALEXANDER ZEMLIANICHENKO/AFP/Getty Images; page 39, DMITRY ASTAKHOV/AFP/Getty Images; page 47, ALEXEI NIKOLSKY/AFP/Getty Images; page 55, Alexsey Druginyn/AFP/Getty Images; page 59, Mikhail Svetlov/Getty Images; page 67, DMITRY ASTAKHOV/AFP/Getty Images; page 71, BRENDAN SMIALOWSKI/AFP/Getty Images; page 87, VLADIMIR RODIONOV/AFP/Getty Images; page 95, ALEXEY NIKOLSKY/AFP/Getty Images.

# QUOTE REFERENCES

**Page 6**
Annual Q & A session with the Russian public, Moscow, Russia, News Blog, *The Guardian* (15 December 2011)

**Page 10**
From a speech at the opening of the Barmaley Fountain in Volgograd, Russia (23 August 2013), *The World According to Vladimir Putin* by Simon Shuster, *Time* (16 September 2013)

**Page 14**
Annual state of the nation address, Moscow, Russia (10 May 2006), *Putin lashes out at 'wolf-like' America* by Nick Paton Walsh, *The Guardian* (11 May 2006)

**Page 18**
*A Plea for Caution From Russia* by Vladimir Putin, *The New York Times* (12 September 2013)

**Page 22**
From a speech at an FSB gala (December 2005), *A Chill in the Moscow Air* by Anna Nemtsova, *Newsweek* (5 February 2006)

**Page 26**
From an interview with Armin Wolf broadcast on Austrian ORF television channel (4 June 2018)

**Page 30**
From the interview *One-on-One With Vladimir Putin* by Gayne C. Young, *Outdoor Life* (17 May 2011)

**Page 34**
From *When Naomi Campbell interviewed Vladimir Putin* by Naomi Campbell (November 2010), *GQ* (11 November 2017, originally published March 2011)

**Page 38**
From an interview given to Luciano Fontana, *Il Corriere della Sera* (6 June 2015)

**Page 42**
Annual press conference, Moscow, Russia (February 2008), *The Truth About Putin and Medvedev* by Amy Knight, *The New York Review of Books* (15 May 2008)

**Page 46**
From *A Call From the Kremlin* by Masha Gessen, *The New York Times* (16 September 2012)

**Page 50**
Annual Q & A session with the Russian public, Moscow, Russia, *Vladimir Putin outdoes himself with 'record-making' televised Q&A*, by Miriam Elder, *The Guardian* (25 April 2013)

**Page 54**
Said in 2012, when asked why he seemed to prefer the company of endangered tigers to his cabinet minister, Fifteen years of Vladimir Putin: in quotes by Roland Oliphant, *The Telegraph* (7 May 2015)

**Page 58**
From an interview with David Miller, London, UK, *USA Today* (5 May 2017)

**Page 62**
Addressing the meeting of the Valdai International Discussion Club, Valdai, Russia, (24 October 2014)

**Page 66**
Addressing the meeting of the Valdai International Discussion Club, Valdai, Russia (19 September 2013)

**Page 70**
Comment made at a press conference after Trump and Putin meeting during the G20 in Hamburg, Germany (7 July 2017)

**Page 74**
Addressing the meeting of the Valdai International Discussion Club, Valdai, Russia (22 October 2015)

**Page 78**
Said in an interview aired by Swiss broadcaster RTS, Geneva, Switzerland (20 July 2015), *People like Blatter deserve Nobel prize, Putin tells Swiss TV* by Tom Miles, Reuters (27 July 2015)

**Page 82**
From the annual press conference, Kremlin, Moscow, Russia, www.en.kremlin.eu (14 February 2008)

**Page 86**
Press conference by President Bush and Russian Federation President Putin, Brdo Castle, Brdo Pri Kranju, Slovenia, https://georgewbush-whitehouse.archives.gov/news/releases/2001/06/20010618.html (16 June 2001)

**Page 90**
From the interview *One-on-One With Vladimir Putin* by Gayne C. Young, *Outdoor Life* (17 May 2011)

**Page 94**
From an interview given to Luciano Fontana, *Il Corriere della Sera* (6 June 2015)